Leaving

Gary

John Sheehan

TIA CHUCHA PRESS
CHICAGO

For Margie and For Ollie

In their style
so different
in their love
so alike

Printed in the United States of America

ISBN 1-882688-16-3
Library of Congress Number: 97-61749

Book design: Jane Brunette
Front cover photo: Paul D. Schneider
Author photo: Kurt Heinz
Project manager: Hugh Steinberg

PUBLISHED BY:
TIA CHUCHA PRESS
A Project of the Guild Complex
PO Box 476969
Chicago, IL 60647

DISTRIBUTED BY:
NORTHWESTERN UNIVERSITY PRESS
Chicago Distribution Center
11030 S. Langley
Chicago, IL 60628

Funding for this project was partially provided by the National Endowment for the Arts, the Illinois Arts Council, and the Lannan Foundation.

ACKNOWLEDGMENTS

"At Old Sylvan Beach," "Riding Down to Galveston," "Coca Cocá Cocá Colá," "Thoughts on Sloth and Mardi Gras," "Comfort of Pumpkins," and "Good Friday" appeared in *Spirits* (Ind. Univ. Northw.) "You Just Can't Be Nice to Some People" appeared in *Indiannual* and *Elsewhere Indiana*. "Terri's Feet" and "Jazz Us Some Language" appeared in *Nit and Wit* and *Elsewhere*. "We've Only Been Messing Up These Dunes," "For Hidden Lake Anthology," "Gary Postscript," "Middlemix U.S.A.," "Maxwell Street Market," "Schoolscape," "No History in Their Bones," "Aftermath," "The Tooth of the Lion," "Give Us This Day," and "The Old Lady's House" appeared in *Elsewhere*. "Steel Country U.S.A." appeared in *Indiannual, Transport Fleet News* and *Elsewhere*. "The Easiest Route to Chicago" and "Jesus Ain't No" appeared in *Skylark* (Purdue Univ. Cal.) and *Elsewhere*. "The Farthest West You Can Go" appeared in *Nit and Wit*. "Color Us Human" appeared in *Skylark*. "On Being Unpublished" appeared in *Soundings*. "By Any Other Name" appeared in *Lucky Star, Whitewater Woman, Indiannual and Elsewhere*. "Thoughts on Sloth and Mardi Gras," "Nanook of the North," "Thoughts of an Ambivalent Carnivore," and "I'm Afraid My Fears Are Just Too Damned Boring" were written for performances by the Chicago Poetry Ensemble.

THANKS : Above all to Margie and Ollie, and then to Shawn. They listened, offered suggestions, encouraged, and even, for the most part, put up with me patiently.

Thanks to Charlie Tinkham, Evangeline Morse, Betty Balog, Jesse Gutierrez, Judy Birch, Amy Garza, Sally Nalbors, Brenda McDade, Tony Fitzpatrick, Julie Parson, Mary Shen Barnidge, Lisa Buscani, Carol Spelius, Agnes Tatara, June Shipley, Mary Le Van, Elizabeth Eddy, Bernard Hillila, Maureen Connelly, Judy Cermick, Debbie Ekdahl, Cheryl Watkins, Jim Gordon, Bill Buckley, Rod Warien and many others in Chicago and N.W. Indiana, who helped and encouraged in various ways;

To Marc Smith, who eleven years ago invited me to join his new group, which became the Chicago Poetry Ensemble, and which performed almost every Sunday night the first year of the Green Mill Poetry Readings, the beginnings of the famous Slam;

To Rob Van Tuyle, who took over as leader of the independent Ensemble and to members and associates Anna Brown, Karen Nystrom, Jean Howard, Joe Virde, Dick McCracken, Dave and Nilla Cooper, Joyce Caskey and Mike Barrett, with special thanks to Rob and Dick for publishing *Elsewhere Indiana;*

To Lew Rosenbaum, Patricia Smith, Michael Warr, and other members of the Guild Complex;

To Luis Rodriguez, Hugh Steinberg, and others of the Tia Chucha Press, for getting this book published;

To Kurt Heinz for the photograph.

Table of Contents

3. Who is my brother, my sister, myself?

4. One Spirit Uniting

LEAVING GARY

I never thought I'd be moving to Portage. But I never thought Margie would have a stroke, nor that my arthritis would get so bad, So I'm in this apartment without any steps, a mile down the road from the nursing home, where I visit Margie every day.

But leaving Gary—

I feel like I'm betraying her. I came to identify so much with her: this ill conceived steel mill mismatched city; this scapegoat of our confused society; this city I taught in 19 years, and 6 more part time; this city where students and people accepted me as one of them; this blessed place I could vent my anger in creative ways; where Black folk respected my anger as their own (some students once told me "Mr. Sheehan, when you get mad you sound Black"); this city where I met and loved Ollie, and after she died got to know and love Margie; this city where I'm known and greeted wherever I go; this city I've loved even more than Chicago; this enchanted place where 1906 and after have not completely destroyed the woods and swamps and dunes of centuries; this Potawatamic crossing grounds; this polluted heaven by hidden lake (but on Clark Road on the west and in Woodlake on the east I never smelled the pollution).

O Gary, heart of our mixed up country, I love you now and forever.

He took us with him

GROWING UP CATHOLIC

The choir sang baroque at Annunciation,
that stately old stucco church,
out of date in the '30s.

Cherubs and saints;
the strictness of God,
leavened by the mercy of his mother;
"How can God have a mother?" I thought.
leavened by the Child,
the shepherds,
the Magi.

The church I grew up in
I've always loved,
because the church I grew up in
loved me.

The laughing sisters of Incarnate Word,
those dancing daughters of God:

Mother Scholastica smiled primly,
Mother Angelique laughed teasingly,
and Mother Gertrude,
that chubby figurine
of an impish Irish aristocrat
peasant,
told me once to pray for my Aunt Mary,
Sister Agatha,
because she was so smart
it got her in trouble.

Mother Gertrude,
that rosy cherub,
who told us not to worry

about being perfect,
because even Ivory soap
was only 99 and 44 hundredths pure.

Mother Gertrude embodied the Spirit,
incarnated the Word,
enfleshed the Wonder
of everydayness
I grew up in.

Then came the Basilians,
priests of St. Basil,
Basilian Fathers
(un-American name,
like nuts from South America),
those down to earth
Canadian Basilians,
who brought hockey to Houston,
and humor to high school classrooms.

Oh the fear of hell was there all right,
warded off by scapular medals,
the nine first Fridays,
and confession at least once a week.

But in all this Romish rigor,
this Tridentine insistence,
was the salt and the savor,
the bread and the wine,
the laughter of common humanity.

Faith of my fathers,
faith of my mothers,
my sister, my brothers,
my wives,
Methodist, Baptist,
as well as Catholic,
I may not believe
like I used to, exactly,
but you taught me to love,
and I love you.

HOUSTON SUMMER '28

We'd sit in the porch swing
savor the shade
swat mosquitoes
watch the slow
parade of cars
going up and down
Main Street

Hudsons and Reos and Model T's
Essex and Whippet
the odd Pierce Arrow
and more Model T's

if you got the swing to yourself
you could stretch out
cautiously though
to keep corners and angles
from hurting your shoulders and back

when evening came
with its breeze from the Gulf
we'd sit there for hours
talking and listening
or just sitting and swatting
until we could go to bed
without sweating up the sheets

one night we sat on the steps
around our neighbors' radio
to hear
the Dempsey-Tunney
championship fight

that was the summer
the Democrats held
their convention in Houston
and the great wooden hall was built
on the edge of downtown
by Buffalo Bayou

we took in two delegates
as boarders
a man and his wife
and we had fried chicken
and ice cream
when it wasn t even Sunday

I yelled out the window
"Hooray for Al Smith!"

Main Street was still Main Street
in '28
some white wooden mansions still stood
with columns and porches
awnings and shrubs
luxuriant stretches of green

but commercial was already spreading

across the street
was a tall thin house
yellow with brown wooden shutters
and a fenced in garden
where two old ladies
worked over the flowers

just south of this house
was the Pig 'n Whistle
a barbecue drive-in
its aroma tickled our nostrils
through the heavy afternoon heat

across from the drive-in
on the corner where streetcars passed
was Le Blanc's Fried Chicken
full meals served up southern style

I used to walk down the oyster-shell alley
to watch the customers go in
to LeBlanc's
and to whiff that frying chicken

stepping gingerly over the shells
to keep from cutting my feet

we had to be careful too
on the sidewalk
to avoid the hot melted tar
in the cracks

we took the streetcar one night
downtown to a picture
and vaudeville show
at the Majestic
the marquee and the lobby
the circular stairs to the balcony
the Oriental walls
in the dimly lit darkness
entranced even more than the movie

on the way home we stopped
for an ice cream soda
I've always remembered the luxury
sitting there in that fancy
confectionary
in a delicate chair
at a delicate table
delicately dipping
the long thin spoon
past cherry

through whipped cream
soda and ice cream
down to the strawberry syrup

in the summer
in Houston
we expected to sweat
but relief had touches
of heaven

QUIET PIANO REVERIE

She played the piano
once
on the radio,

And I had never seen her playing it at home at all.

I wondered why it was important
to my mother and my aunt
that Grandma should play the piano
over the radio.

We went next door to listen.
It was tinkly and quiet and slow.

I've heard those sounds in jazz and classical
over the years,
from distant rooms,
on lazy afternoons.

I hear them from the radio now,
as I idle the winter morning,
gazing at the fireplace,
the photos on the mantle,
the sunlit curtains.

WORLDS APART

I.

Grandma would sit in her rocker for hours
hardly saying a word

but she took us for walks
or to movies
she told us stories
she heard my catechism lessons
(she said sácrifice instead of sacrifíce)

I worried about her Methodist soul
how could she be invincibly ignorant
but she'd never become a Catholic

when I was fifteen
she took to talking a lot
cooked a meal again after twenty years
and went out to make converts of her own
for the Townsend Old Age Pension Plan

she gave me a copy of a prayer she wrote
"that all may be one in the Spirit"
it scared me and I burned it

they had to take her away
two hundred miles
to the state hospital

in a year she was dead
no one of her family was there

II.
twenty years later
I was substitute priest
at a Veterans' Hospital one Sunday

be cool but cautious
they'd told me
so Saturday night I made sure
I was safely locked in
the chaplain's apartment
and set the clock for 5:30

at 6 in the morning I unlocked the door
looked cautiously out and stepped into the cold

at the main building a guard let me in
and led me down two hallways
unlocking and relocking each door
then a patient took over
and led me down more corridors
unlocking relocking each door

I too was a prisoner
but my guides were friendly
their greetings as warm and as safe as the halls

the congregation was small
about fifty
quiet with just a few restless stirrings
they listened attentively
as I preached on love
and understanding
nothing to upset them

in the sacristy and in the dining hall
where about three hundred ate quietly
everyone was pleasant and kind

I couldn't tell the guards from the patients

it was only on the bus
heading for home
that I began to feel strange
about where I had been.
the rudeness of the driver
and the complaints of the riders
made me feel at home

      III.
I've often wondered
how my grandmother died
was she calm and peaceful
like those patients I saw?
or was she in another part of the hospital?

I wish I had kept her prayer

AT OLD SYLVAN BEACH

Galveston Bay, Summer 1930

The well-trodden grass runs to brown
cows flap their tails against the flies

my brother and I in faded overalls
pick our barefoot way around dung piles
past stacks of rotting wood
and turned-over rowboats
towards the rickety pier
that stretches out in the bay

people dangle their legs over the sides
holding strings down for crabs

the sun beats hot through our shirts
and the pier burns our feet
we need to get into the shade

so we make our way back
gingerly stepping
across the oyster shell beach
to the grass

we sit against a live oak tree
and watch ants at work in the dust

the salt air is heavy
with the smell of tar and dead fish

in the distance we see a ship
slowly approaching the channel

we wish we had nickels
for strawberry sodas

but when evening comes
and the breezes blow
we can put on our suits
and wade carefully out
squishing the mud through our toes

BROOKSIE

The first lady we called on
that winter Sunday afternoon
a few months after my mother died
served us cookies and lemonade
her father showed us the intricate figures
he made out of nutshells and wire
she was a junior high school teacher
prim and proper
we never saw her again

our second stop was at Ann Wyse's house
she and her friends were playing bridge
in her cluttered living room
knickknacks end tables souvenirs
and two jars full of candy

Brooksie came bouncing in from a back room
wearing a robe and fluffy slippers
she greeted us warmly
she was an unmarried school teacher too
kindergarten and first grade
we stayed quite a while
and by the time we left
the candy jars were empty

Dad took us back many times to see Brooksie
we took her to restaurants
she came with us on picnics
sometimes he went alone to see her
in about five months they were married

I could not call her "Mother" at first
but before I knew it I could

Brooksie had a Chevrolet coupe that shimmied
Dad used to prop up the trunk
so my brothers and I could ride back there
when we went to Spring Creek for swimming

she brought a small library to our house
including stuff from her trip to France
I especially remember the postcard copies
of famous paintings in the Louvre
several of them were of naked ladies
reclining in fancy boudoirs
she also had stacks of National Geographic
I'd show them to my friends
and was going to start a lending library

Brooksie didn't eat any Sunday night supper
but we soon got her used to it
Dad taught her to make sandwiches
from the beef left over from dinner
he also taught her to cook
she became pretty good at it
but he usually fixed the Sunday roast

Dad had learned to cook
from his German Jewish mother
and he loved to cook all his life
he didn't much like selling cars though
and he didn't sell many
he drank too much
Brooksie continued teaching

in three years my sister Pat was born
a phenomenon in our family
a sister
and red headed
I was fourteen

Dad kept drinking
Mother hugged me one day

and told me she might have to leave

but one evening a few months later
on the living room couch
Dad seemed to have his arms around
all of us at once
he was crying
he told us he needed our help
after that he improved a little

I used to sometimes think I should pray
for him to have a happy death
so life would be easier for the rest of us

I delivered The Houston Chronicle
afternoons and Sunday mornings
Dad helped with the heavy Sunday ones
he'd drag me out of bed at four o'clock
and drive me to the pick-up corner
where we waited sleepy-eyed for the papers
we'd stack them in the back seat
he'd drive while I delivered
several houses each stop
we'd get back home by daylight

I'd fall into bed and sleep until ten
then walk to St. Anne s for Mass
and when I got home I could smell dinner cooking

much of the 35 dollars a month
I made from the paper route
went to my parents for groceries
by the time I quit to go Toronto
I'd contributed 500 dollars
years later after my father had died
and I had married
Brooksie gradually paid all of it back
as if she owed it

Dad improved much more before he died
the last 8 years of life
if he drank at all
it was very rarely
he'd drive Mother to school every day
then go home and clean the house
he'd work in the yard
or at his carpenter's bench
fix supper and go get Mother

Brooksie never became a Catholic
like my Methodist first mother Florence had
but remained a hardshell Baptist all her life
she wouldn't let Pat go to Catholic school
like Bill and Holley and I did
but Pat went to Brooksie's grade school
and then to public high

but she sent Pat faithfully
to Mass with us
and for weekly religious instruction
sometimes Mother would come with us to Mass
but we never set foot in the Baptist church
so strict was ours back then

up until the time I was ordained
I worried about Brooksie's salvation
and prayed she d become a Catholic
but my theology broadened
and I came to believe
that an all-wise all-good all-powerful God
could not possibly punish forever
millions and millions of people
who either had not heard
or could not believe
that the holy Roman Catholic Apostolic Church
was the one true way to heaven
I stopped worrying about that
and started worrying about other things

Brooksie tried to love Ollie
when I shocked them all
after 21 years of priesthood
by getting married
but though she wrote
and sent us gifts
and even spoke with Ollie on the phone
she could not bring herself to meet Ollie

it bothered her a lot I think
that she could not break the racial bind

before she died a few years later
I visited her with Ollie's blessing

one odd thing
with all the changes of the '60s and on
Pat is the one of us
who's most completely an orthodox Catholic

Pat like Holley
visited Ollie before she died
and is now warm friends with Margie

Margie's Black Baptist church
has a different style
from the White one Brooksie attended
but their basic beliefs are the same
and not that much different from Catholic

I'm still a Catholic
ecumenical
radical
hoping for changes

if I could only be as ecumenical
politically as I am religiously

SPOILED BY TORONTO

I was spoiled by Toronto
it was so humane
no typing required
nor hardly any papers

the best that church and state could give
for free

we only paid with our lives

St. Michael's College
in the U. of Toronto
those sons of Irish immigrants
suddenly peers
of Anglican gentry

free to walk those lordly halls
use every library
enjoy the tradition and prestige
of academia

the best of Rome and the best of Oxford
Sarbonne and Bologna
Louvain and Harvard

Aristotle and Aquinas
updated and made respectable
by Maritain and Gilson

we breathed a privileged air
and our meals were steady

but still we could boast
we were true to the Gospel

with Vincent de Paul
and Dorothy Day

after all
we only drew
two dollars a week
for spending money
and the meals were not all that good

but within the limits of clerical discipline
we had plenty of room to roam
joking wildly if not forgetting
the grosser demands of the body

within the limits of Catholic doctrine
the wide world's delights were ours

nature and art
school and town
valley and market and street

lecture hall library gallery

the main luxury was all that leisure
all that security
three squares and a roof
clothes enough and medical care
no worries no bills

just keep the rule
say your prayers
pass the exams

and let your mind wander
through all those books
those places those centuries
those ever recurring springs
those ancient worlds and new

CONSIDER

how we seldom consider
I mean sit down and think
let our minds wander
wherever they will
without any audio-visuals

in the forties I used to ride the train
every two summers
between Toronto and Houston
black suit and tie
seminary rule

I'd find a seat
and put up my luggage
plop down and loosen my tie
look over the paper or magazine
look up and around at the people
see if the window would open
light up a cigarette
luxuriate
in the freedom
sometimes I'd take off the tie

no one could bother me for two whole days
I could read and think and observe
my butt would get sore
but I could get up and walk
the length of the train
stop at the diner
or even the club car
study the other passengers

In the fifties I went home every summer
tie gave way to Roman collar

a magnet for Catholic drunks
for them a sign from heaven
so I usually took off the collar

but not every drinker was drunk
the collar could be an advantage
free drinks and dinners
interesting conversation
"It's not the humidity, it's the stupidity,"
was told me of Texas by a man from Seattle

I later learned
in Rochester, Chicago and Indiana
that northern veneer can fool you
civilization is not always
what we were taught to think

Chicago back then was 12th Street Station
crowds and lines for Parmalee
to get to another depot
sometimes there were several hours
I'd walk down Michigan Avenue
explore the loop
once I went to a stage show
saw Bob Hope
it gave me a worldly feeling

consider the Saturday Evening Post
the good life was less expensive then
for those of us who belonged
to the club sandwiches
on Walgreen s balcony

as we slowly pulled into Houston
the skyline would gleam in the distance
while the immediate view
was unpainted shanties
and bayou greenery

consider the meaning of World War II
Hitler was more us than we suspected
there was a story in the *New Yorker*
about soldiers on furlough in Alabama
who had to eat in the kitchen
because they were Black
while German prisoners
dined in the main room

I read that story riding the train

Consider too much it will get you in trouble
it's safer to watch T.V.

RIDING DOWN TO GALVESTON
1950S SUMMERS

Hot feet Houston   creosote   pine
Pasadena fogfart   rotten eggs   paper mills
fills nostrils
clean rain   westwind   sunglare
warms   dries
shirt flapping breeze
freeway expressway   zoomaway
for GALVESTON

flat road   signboards   prairie
f l a t
rice swamp   grassbirds   signboards   cattle
cold war chemicals
nasal sting
c l e a r   s t r e t c h e s
grass
f l a t f l a t f l a t
to the causeway
over water   brown water
fishing boats

G A L V E S T O N

NEON   FINE FOODS
ICE COLD BEER
EATS
boulevard   palm trees
stilt houses   mansions
peeling paint   shutters

bayous   bridges
boating   bait

shrimpstink   fresh salt
stale water   oil

SEAWALL
boulevard   misty spray
salt water   seagulls   souvenirs
BIKINI
suntan   cotton candy
hamburgers   shells
fancy dingy old hotels
slick motels

SOUPWATER ROLLING
sunglare   daze
itchy   sweat
mosquitoes   scratch
shower two bits

The best things in life cost 25 cents
in Galveston Texas 1950s

CELIBATE NERVES

music records   FM radio
smooth and soothing
for celibate nerves

but Beethoven Bach and Brahms
boring after a while
too Platonic
Aristotelian
neat
want tribal drums and peasant dance
slavic Congo Mongol sweep
welcome cacophony
of sage and savage culture

dig deep to find the healing roots
bitter wine better than sweet

YOU JUST CAN'T BE NICE TO SOME PEOPLE

My wife was the only Black at the wedding.
They were affluent, liberal Catholics,
We stayed late;
just a few drinkers left.
A pious old Irishman
turned benignly and said,
"I love all Negroes."
But she shot back,
"Why you son of a bitch,
I can't stand half the motherfuckers myself."

EPITHALAMION

I hear the touch of your reality
more than I could ever see it.
I hear your stillness,
feel your heartbeat,
know your inmost soul.
You refresh me into a lover,
momentarily real,
forever rising from the grave
to Hallelujah laughter
of our grandchildren.

I awake in startled amazement
observing your delicate toughness.
Your dust dances in the sun.
Tatterdemalion perfection in your old cotton vatin.

Our love grows strong on mutual outrage.
We surprise ourselves bending with joy to each other.
Our abiding contradicts the encounter.

TERRI'S FEET

Terri's feet are just like mine
but smaller browner smoother
smell different
but sometimes the same
five toes on each foot
but she ain't got no hammer toe

she loves to take off her shoes
and dance and wade
and splash in the water

and that's the way it would be
even if she
were Vietnamese or Congolese or Viennese
or Irish
and I were Japanese or Pekinese or Siamese
or Eskimo

as it is she's Afro- and I'm Euro-
American
but not really

she's Terri and I'm John
her Nana is my wife Ollie
and that's that

FOR MARGIE

With all these ailments,
what's she got going for her?

Besides
that smile
that sneaks up on me,
that look in her eyes
that surprises,

the way she gets down on paper
the way people talk,
the way she gets down
to the nitty,
when things have gotten
too gritty.

This little girl,
grandmother,
lady who loves,
what's she got going for her?

Just that
her love,
her surprise.

And with that she's got me.
I go for her.

SHE LIKES

Margie likes
Maxwell Street
fleamarkets
resales
sales

North Michigan Avenue

children
church
soft music
Gospel
just about everybody she meets

phone calls
snapshots
city lights

the scenic route to Chicago

doodads
thingamajigs
antiques
junk

her taste is eclectic
sometimes discerning

she even likes me
most of the time

I'M AFRAID MY FEARS ARE JUST TOO DAMNED BORING

I'm afraid my fears are just too damned boring.
I can't express them in an entertaining way.
And I seem to be too narcissistic
to make up outrageous stories,
or even report on real ones.

Too wrapped up in my own
getting up in the morning fears,
going to bed at night fears,
getting old fears,
poor performance fears,
no performance fears,

car won't start,
bills won't get paid
fears,
writer's block,
Alzheimer fears,
track and retrack
10,000 wrong turn
fears,

papers piling up,
letters unanswered,
junk mail unsorted.

Some of it makes me feel guilty.
Some of it makes me more scared.

I'm afraid I'll never get it said,
and if I say it
it won't be heard,
and if it's heard
it won't be understood,

or appreciated,
or applauded.

Applause!
That's what I'm hooked on.
It's easier than love.
But I want applause
for my whole damned life,
for the meaning that doesn't get into the words.

If only I'd learned to listen more
to some who listened to me

I'm afraid the whole conversation
will dwindle and die,
and I'll still be trying to start it.

MEMORIAL DAY 1984
ABOUT 7:00 A.M.

On looking at book, ENCOUNTER WITH ART, "The artist looks at his world."

I look up at this room
with its symbols its memories
family photos on mantle
under library print
of old English landscape
that fits this house
the drapes and furniture
she carefully chose
the fireplace we loved
and seldom used

there are not enough quiet moments
to savor to trouble to rearrange
outer and inner reality
fantasy
making up making do making over
house into home into wide wide world
into art and a brand new reality
growing out of the old

I think some times the old beliefs
have to be true at least partly

this house is still so beautiful
Ollie
that I believe you still exist
in a good and somehow living way
in the all-pervading Spirit
the Spirit my grandmother prayed for
those uneasy years before she died
the spirit that filled me long ago

in the brownwood basement chapel
of St. Michael's College Toronto
the spirit I felt on the ferry boat
to Staten Island
one starry night
the summer I was ordained

one Spirit uniting
the whole human family

right here
in this chapel
in this living room
in every scared scarred sacred
person
who ever existed or will

2.

This

Duneswamp

Woodlake

Steelsmoke

Region

WE'VE ONLY BEEN MESSING UP THESE DUNES SINCE 1906

How can all this foliage grow on sand?
I had always thought dunes would be sand sand
like desert or beach sand
non-life
or hardly at all

but this sand supports all kinds of life
and death
since the iron age
the steel age
the garb-age
started

death and life
in strange of nature and man's motive marriage mixed

many people have lived in Gary all their lives
hardly knowing the lake is there
behind the mills
the big lake that made the dunes
the life
is hidden from the people.

EPITHETS AND EPITAPHS
STEEL COUNTRY U.S.A.

Indiana
is not an "Indian" name,

nor even is Calumet,
but a French name
for the "Indian" peace pipe.

Chicago is "Indian" though—
Eschicagou, onion swamp.

Jean Baptiste Pointe du Sable
is the French name
of a Black man,
a voyageur,
who first after the "Indians"
settled Chicagoland, the Calumet.

Indians?
The people:
Potawatomi, Miami, Ottawa,
Illinois, Menomenee,
and others
lived in this region.

Uncivilized,
backward,
deprived,
they had their ritual
Pipe of Peace.

We have steelsmoke,
expressway smoke,

cigarette smoke,
gunsmoke,
bombsmoke.

INDIAN SAVAGES,
you can have your country back.
We 've used it up,
and are moving to the moon.

FOR HIDDEN LAKE ANTHOLOGY
GARY, INDIANA, 1978

I hadn't thought to go to the funeral
or even the wake
of Johnny B.
I hadn't really known him
that well
he'd only attended two classes
back in September
then skipped the rest of the year

but his friends are my friends
they call me brother
they call me cool

and then I remembered
three Junes ago
in the cottage "portable"
where I taught then
he and a couple of others
stopped by to chat
while I was marking papers

and Johnny
though he couldn't possibly pass
he'd skipped most of that year too
wrote me a page
on his that day's activities

bicycling around
bugging teachers and guards
being chased there to here

well he didn't bug me
though his friends often did

in their friendly way
the ones who came to class

so I slipped into the funeral home
to pay my respects
to a sixteen year old adult
tough
disillusioned
wearing shades in the coffin
the Brotherhood emblem
"Sworn to Fun"
draped overhead
loyal
to the end
that came too soon
shot dead
by a brother
of a different hood

GARY POSTSCRIPT '89

The "urban renewal" is still a wasteland
downtown is well-kept ruins
boarded-up buildings abound
groups have been formed to take action

but most of the city's a garden
woods and dunes pervade it
the trash is only along the edges

get off the main streets
and you'll be surprised
by the neatness
the everyday ordinariness
children playing
lawnmowers humming
mothers unafraid

the schools I taught in were noisy but friendly
the jiving was mainly merriment
the gangs mostly clubs
the learning more than you'd think

though six of my students were shot to death
out of six thousand

I've lived in this house for sixteen years
I walk the dog down the street to the woods
kids and their parents call me by name
for better or worse Gary's my home
and I'd rather live in this left-over city
than in any suburb I know

ALTERNATE VIEW

I.

The new Post-Tribune
screams
like The Region
like the signs on Highway 30
a clutter of colors
and titillations
a new sensation
every flick of the eye
sight-bites to catch consumers

but forget the paper
forget TV
forget bargains and stop-lights and trucks

there still lurk dunes
and swamps and farmland
orchards and gardens and fishing ponds

I don't see chicken-yards anymore
but I've seen a few horses
and even some cows

more squirrels than rats
run in our alley
maybe because of the cats
that I made the mistake of feeding

twice this summer I saw deer
once right here in Gary

II.

in the swamp down the street
next to the woods where the old Slavic lady

tended her herbs and her flowers
a pond appears every March or April
with frogs and a pair of ducks

by May they've all disappeared
but violets cover
the patches of sunlight

later come blackberries
and changes of flowers right into November

once in a while I see a bloom
left over from the lady's garden
the only signs that her house was once there

folks still fish the polluted waters
the swans on Wolf Lake
don't know we're endangered

MIDDLEMIX USA

This hodgepodge gardenfarm lakemill region
this duneswamp woodstown tangle of tracks
this polyglot dumping ground
this trucking capital of the nation
this segregated polarized mixture
of wonderment and frustration
conflict and hospitality
this sanctuary of diversity

we got the biggest soap factory in the world
the easiest route to Chicago
the most civilized low priced movie house
in the country
(there's an intermission with coffee and cake)
the last surviving interurban trolley
the most hidden politics in the country
the most fragmented population

most of our news from Chicago
our economy tied to Chicago
we're Chicago's industrial hinterland
we know more about Illinois than we do about Indiana

we got nudist colonies to the south of us
vice from the heyday of Al Capone
dope peddling to rival anywhere

aging hippies bikers idealists
activists socialists
fundamentalist kooks

people who run away and don't want to come back
people who move here and are enchanted

hustlers after the American dream
hustlers chasing a different dream

escape artists
tattoo artists
refugees from the mainstream

some of the loveliest beaches
the richest farmland
a gardener's paradise
a naturalist's delight

a plethora of video
hardly any bookstores

and Sears and Roebuck love us all

THE EASIEST ROUTE
TO CHICAGO FROM GARY

I used to take the expressway
but trucks and repair work took over
and tollroad is too expensive
so now I take the scenic route
by the lake
through the mills
the old ethnic mix

I turn north up the ramp
and take off on Cline
quick-glimpsing the lake
past "Roman" ruins
arched "aqueduct"
"viaduct"
ore-duct

I glide by towers and chimneys
a dreamlike steelscape
of monster machines
on the other side roofs
of East Chicago and Hammond

then curve down
through fumes of refineries
to the enclave of Whiting

past huge slavic churches
the Faith triumphant
bay windows
pubs
weathered brick fronts
1900s surviving

I pick up speed and cross the state line
past restaurants
and cigarette liquor bargains
approaching the entrance to tollroad bridge
that arches over the traffic and grime
of Polish town steel town East Side
unassimilated chunk of Chicago

I turn under the tollroad
hugging the lake
a few blocks to the right
hidden by working class homes
Serbo-Croatian
restaurants closed down
but bars and fast food still open
Slavic is mixed with Latino
peppered lightly with Black

more bay windows
Victorian fronts
outside stairs
like Galveston
or New Orleans
you step down a story
from street to yard

I cross the drawbridge
over Calumet Harbor
glancing quickly
for ships from the ocean

rust piles salt piles
gravel
wrecked cars
huddle around the harbor

another huge church
looms ahead

its back right up to the walls
of the vast empty mill

houses packed snugly around
pour children onto the streets
with old survivors
and jobless young

continuing north
I drive between rows
of duplex apartments

then highrises mingling with mansions
1900s homes
1920s apartments Italian style
the Black bourgeoisie
a few lingering Whites
liberals
intellectuals
or just plain stuck

a sharp turn
past the country club
a landmark kept up for the people
I swerve by marinas
the boats of the rich
through Jackson Park
by Wooded Island
and science museum
Chicago a garden
along the lake

I turn west under the railroad tracks
into the Plaisance
the wide boulevard
that leads to the great university
this Hyde Park mecca
of culture and beauty

this ambivalent force
that unites and divides
the Calumet region
this Alma Mater
of the giant bomb

MAXWELL STREET MARKET

Sunday morning
Chicago
people promenade
in the ruins of the city
cars inch honking through the crowds
old folks young folks
hip bedraggled
dressed undressed
rags regalia
all styles of living unafraid
friendly
at least not very hostile
an ounce of trust to a pound of caution
curiosity spices the scene
cats of all colors come out
enjoy the crowd the merchandise
tawdry gaudy cheap and lively
the healthy smell of deft survivors
the grace the wit the grit the savor
of bleak salvation from Saturday night
risk ten cents for recompense
or a hundred dollars
but don't ask where it comes from
is the fresh fruit a rotten bargain?
tacos sausage pig ears ribs
hot off the smoking grill
blues and jazz and raucous rock
old time jumping gospel
junk hides many a lucky find
the city is whole in this holy place
old ladies and children are safe
in the jampacked crowds
of Maxwell Street Market
Sunday morning
Chicago

SCHOOLSCAPE

The scene
can we make it?
these books are so heavy
how can we float on the poetry of Shakespeare?

the sun
is five days early
for spring
we'll run out in the yard
and into the street
light up our oatmeal
and smoke us some poetry
we'll patch up the buildings with posters

we'll dance on the beach
study the sand
the windblown seeds
succession of life

we'll speed on the throughway
escape trucks and cops
land in a ditch
to nurse our wounds
and return to the solace of Shakespeare

why is it that he
of all the tragedians
mixes in comedy most?

Shakespeare the Beatles and Jesus
will live on forever with jazz

we 'll jive up some Shakespeare

try it in the classroom
play it in the park
take it to the streets
and civilize the city
high on the depths
of imagined reality

sip sap supper sapientia
wisdom
savory saving salt

3.

Who
is my
brother,
my
sister,
myself?

SONG FOR THE NINETIES

Beware of the Arab, beware of the Jew,
beware of the English, the Irish,
the Tutsi, the Hutu,
the Serbs, the Croatians,
beware of the born-again Christian.

Beware of the Black, beware of the White,
beware of the students, the teachers,
the old, the young,
the rich, the poor,
beware the wild Indian swinging his tomahawk.

Beware the Catholic, beware the Protestant,
the atheist, the agnostic,
Beware the criminal, beware the police.
beware of your friendly protectors,
the status quo, the avante garde,
beware the revolution.

Beware of the devil who lies inside
your brother, your sister, yourself.

Beware of talking with any of these,
but beware the more if there is no talk.

Just beware, Baby, beware.

NO HISTORY IN THEIR BONES

These northern Whites,
did all their grandparents
just come over in 1912?
The mills, big steel, tin Lizzie, big Mack,
a Ford in your future,
and ten thousand trucks?

Yes, Virginia,
there was a pre-industrial America,
the sweat, the grit, the delicate skill,
cotton and lumber and brick.
Trains to Chicago came from someplace;
trains from Chicago went someplace,
even beyond St. Louis and Detroit and Cleveland,
like Hearne, Texas,
where one railroad met the mud,
or Houston,
where seventeen met the sea,
the sluggish, muddy Gulf,
salty and soothing and healing,
for limbs and heads that ached from history.

As a very small kid in Los Angeles,
I remember seeing only one Black person,
Negro then,
a large woman,
to fit the stereotype,
but back in Ventura,
when I was two,
this little girl,
with pigtails, and a wagon like mine,
stood there beckoning,
not in her mind, maybe,
but in mine.

When we moved back from California to Houston,
we saw them on the streetcars,
3/5 of the seats with "Colored Only,"
we saw them all over Houston.
Niggertown was no inner-city ghetto,
Niggertown was wedges of the pie,
corners and pockets here and there,
peppering the city.

They lived close to where they worked,
to the white kitchens and yards and filling stations.
Many houses had garage apartments for the maids.
The rich had chauffeurs.
We saw them working;
we knew they weren't loafers.
There was no such thing as welfare.
Most of the beggars who came to our door were White.
Any Black man came was asking to do the yard.

We didn t know our Black brothers and sisters and cousins
as well as we might have,
but we knew damned well they worked
for whatever living they got,
and we sensed in our Faulknerian bones
they really were our cousins and sisters and brothers,
no aliens just arrived,
to invade our territory.

History we had down south in our bones,
that never got into the books.

ON THE DEATH OF
LORD LOUIS MOUNTBATTEN

I'm not really glad he died like that
blasted to bits in an Irish bay
but it does seem fitting
him an admiral of the British seas
hero veteran of all those wars

they say he wanted no Japanese
at his funeral
he couldn't forgive them
after all those years

idling away his vacation
on a yacht like that
in the waters of the poor

was his death any sadder
than some tenement kid's
in Dublin or Belfast
Glasgow or London?

Prince Charles read the scriptures beautifully
that highly privileged welfare recipient
and the lines about
"those who go down to the sea in ships"

I'm Irish English German Jewish and French
and likely much more I don't know
but Irish I am in my heart
and though I don't go along with the killing
in my heart I'm a member of the I.R.A.

as I am a Palestinian
Palestinians need homes too

and opposing Israel for your home
does not necessarily make you a Nazi
any more than being Sandinista
makes you anti- or un-American

there are better ways than fighting
but I can understand
why some of the poor
fight the way they do

but then Prince Charles
and the rest of the Mountbatten family
did not entirely choose
their privileged welfare roles

A GOOD YEAR FOR PLASTIC

First there were those ugly pumpkins
that wrinkled and sagged
like moons in a painting by Dali

next those cheap looking Xmas bows
on windows and doors and bushes
wherever a ribbon doesn't belong

then all the yellow ones for the war
like you weren't patriotic
unless you bought at least one

somebody made a lot of money
on America's need for ritual display

almost as much money maybe
as on patriot missiles

I understand wanting
our soldiers home
I wanted them here all along
I support our troops
I'm glad they re safe

But I'm sorry that even so few as 200
got killed over there

I'm sorry 100,000 or so
Iraqui got killed
thousands more sick and dying

Kuwait wasted
all that oil burning
the Gulf polluted

America's soul polluted
dreaming our denial
of guilt over Vietnam

we punished the madman by running amok
and multiplied his damage

now we can look at our own cities
and maybe decide to bomb them too

make America safe for the suburban market
we can really feel good again

THE FARTHEST WEST
YOU CAN GO IS EAST

On John Hersey s War Comment in Newspaper column - 1946

This holy place
this hearthside
this inner citadel
of all we love
you invade at your risk

these icons
you do not defile
these sacred signs
of our own flesh and blood
you keep your foreign hands off

heathen savages
imps from hell
like those buck-toothed
Japanese
the cartoons showed
in the forties

I remember the column
where Hersey described
the lonely corpse
of a brave young soldier
lying on a Pacific beach
treasured contents
of his wallet
all scattered
pictures of sweetheart
of mother and father
of sisters and brothers
souvenirs
of deepest frivolities

all that innocence wasted
an American kid
so far from home

but my eyes grew wider
at the end of the article

the dead soldier
was Japanese
thousands of miles
from his Japanese home
his holy loved ones
Japanese
his roots of reality
Japanese
his tears and laughter
Japanese

NANOOK OF THE NORTH

I saw that movie a hundred times.
Amazing the way that savage
hurried the igloo up,
icy wind stinging his face.
Amazing his sureness of eye and hand
for safety from Arctic night.

The family huddled under furs,
the mother washing her baby with spittle,
chewing to softness her husband's boots,
the boy's delight in castor oil,
the finding and spearing of fish under ice,
the sure-footed stepping from icefloe to icefloe.

Was their survival more savage than mine,
in city classroom,
in truck-jammed traffic,
digging through papers
to deal with deadlines
of friendly bank,
friendly insurance,
friendly federal government?

Nanook s great-grandchildren
don't have to hurry
each day before night.
The trading post has expanded.
They're supplied by air,
civilized by rock and roll.

They can wander the town
in search of their soul,
as modern and free
as a Menominee
on the streets
of Uptown Chicago.

COLOR US HUMAN

The English language
has a natural bias
rooted in its Germanic past
growing later with Latin embellishments
from the sun-dazzled brightness
of the sea-between-lands

Black runs to the bad
as in blackguard and blackmail
black marks on your white shirt
from dirt
black marks on your soul
from sin
but repentance washes it
whiter than snow
(Did the ancient Jews
have a narrow view too?)
the dark Italians they say
preferred blondes
dark clouds mean trouble
there's denigrate and niggardly
"the picture is not completely black"
black vestments for requiem
black garments for mourning
black magic is the evil kind

But then some evil
ain't all that evil
so black can be power
and oil rich as gold
black earth for farming
black stockings for love
in the cool cool dark of the evening

Sophia Loren
brunette beauty
"black *but* beautiful"
was Solomon s love
black hole of love
dark glasses
refreshing shade from the sun
dark wine
caviar
suntan

The practical Nordic
has always preferred
to be in the black
and not in the red

Come close to the carcass
the maggots are white
pale death
ghosts white as a sheet
we blanch with fear
go blank
bland and tasteless
barren sand
freezing snow
blinding sun
yellow pus
yellow piss
pallid and sickly
white hair loss of strength
pale paper substitute
for life
bleached bones
dandruff

White sunburns easier
shows more blemishes
and wrinkles quicker

Wouldn't you think
all that cold northern snow
would make dark winter shelter
welcome and snug
and make black
a more favorable shade?

But it rained more than snowed
on those islands
they were foggy and gray
(parts of Germany too?)
so they prized the rare sunlight
and were bedazzled
as well as enlightened
by the burnished gifts of civilization
borne by dark Romans and Greeks
from their sun-bleached world
its bright shores strewn
with the bones and ruins
of antiquity
sun-washed and whitened

like themselves in their souls
purified
by Plato's meanderings
Aristotle's straight lines
by Apollo the sun God
and Zeus the sky father
who replaced the dark gods
of Old Mother Earth
Dionysus
Aphrodite of the many names
the sprites and nymphs
that dwelt in the deep
ravines of wooded mountains

Do we dig down deep to culture
or scrape the sky
with high civilization's tower of Babel?

I don't understand your language
so it must be crazy
like you and your non-
greenness

I was raised in this pod
and the pod is green
like me and my brothers and sisters
but you ain't green
you're yellow
so go back to your side of the bayou

Black?
ain't no such thing as absolute black
in people
but all shades of darkness blending with light
various browns and yellows and blues
absolute black would be dead

White?
ain't no such thing as absolute white
in people
but all shades of lightness blending with dark
pink and blue and tan and mottled
absolute white would be dead

Rainbow colored was the sign they said
of the calm at the end of the flood
rainbow mixture of darkness and light
is the whole human family
richly fleshed over with varitoned nature
to dance at the wedding of earth and sky
dive deep in the waters of wisdom
leap high with the laughing fire

POLITICAL PRISONERS U.S.A.?
AIN'T NOBODY HERE
BUT US ANTI-SEMANTICS

Polis -   the city
Politics -   the running of the city
                        running for office
                        running around for votes
                        running up the bill
                        running down the other side
                        running from the police
Police -   the city guards
                        who run down those
                        who run into those
                        who run the city
Prison -   where they run the wrong runners
                        of the other side.
                        Wrong runners of our side,
                        the right side, the ruling side,
                        sometimes go to jail,
                        but not quite so often,
                        so easily, so quickly,
                        for so long a stay,
                        and even, if they're right enough,
                        not too badly.
Political Prisoners -   wrong runners, real or suspected,
                        from the wrong side, whose numbers
                        far exceed
                        their real guilt.

I used to visit the Houston jail, every week, to see Joe Brown, 18,
Black. Joe could hardly stay out of jail. As soon as he was out
he'd get picked up again, usually on a Saturday night. He could
hardly stay away from his crowd. The cops got somebody in his
crowd about once a month, and they'd pick up Joe too, as

accomplice, or suspect. Innocent or guilty, Joe couldn't stay out of jail.

The White middle class college students I was teaching at that time seemed to me no better or worse that Joe. On Saturday nights they sometimes got drunk, got in fights, or cheated on money.

But they didn't need to use force or violence. They had the keys; they knew the combination. They were not gathered on crowded corners, outside small stores and hot cafes. They were less densely ensconced in cool bars and clubs, and spacious homes, at beach resorts or country lodges. There were more places for them to safely park, in the dark, more protected than molested by cops.

Was Joe Brown a political prisoner? Is he still one? How many Joe Browns do you think there are in cities like Chicago, or Houston, or Louisville?

Political prisoners U.S.A.? Economic prisoners? Is there a difference?

THOUGHTS OF AN AMBIVALENT CARNIVORE

I could be a vegetarian.
It would probably work for a while.
But what good would it do,
except for my health
and my psyche?

Non-violence can only go so far.

Would I have to stop swatting mosquitoes?
Spraying roaches?
Stepping on ants?

Even Jesus was a fisherman.

Animals kill animals,
without any training from us.

Maybe there was a garden of Eden,
where lions and lambs played harmlessly,
and rabbits snuggled up with dogs.

But every animal goes for food,
where nature tells him to find it.

Christians eat the Body of Christ;
lovers nibble each other;
baby sucks mother's breasts.

We kill one another with kindness.

The old give way to the young;
I'll have to move over.

But please, move me gently.
Don't be in a hurry;
hesitate.

Let me savor these last few
burgers and dogs.

COCA COCÁ COCÁ COLÁ

God saw they were good
wind and water
earth and fire
fish and birds

and crocodiles

trees and bushes and weeds
all seeds thereof
all fruits and berries

and leaves

everything she created was good

every crawling and walking creature
the furry four-legged ones
and the naked two-legged ones
who work and worry
and celebrate
who elaborate their food
pound it
grind it
change it with fire

or let it ferment
and pass it around
on solemn and sacred occasions
in ritual celebration
or routine relaxation

some do it with wine

in Andes and Amazon
they do it with coca
resting from toil
re-creating their spirits

they chew the leaf
and feel free
it is good
it's part of their culture
they've done it for centuries

but the stranger came into their forests
to baptize
civilize
aggrandize
and do a good thing to death
and do a good thing to death
and do a good thing to ten thousand gleams of light
in the eyes of entrepreneurs

AFTERMATH

After math
we'll do physics
and after physics
we'll build a bomb
and after the bomb
there'll be no math

the Indians were poets
the Europeans were scientists
the Indians sang the world
the Europeans measured it

math is a Greek word for knowledge
knowledge is not enough
sophia is a Greek word for wisdom
math measures reality
wisdom dives into it
wisdom revels in reality
wisdom can't help but sing
math is too busy counting

before math marks the final countdown
will wisdom be able to save us?

but aftermath is after mowing
old English Germanic not Greek
the sweet smell of grass and clover

the dead hay makes way for new growth
the roots are still green
they grow into green
oh give us some green
we need new green

One

Spirit

Uniting

THOUGHTS ON SLOTH
AND MARDI GRAS

Shrove Tuesday they called it in chilly England,
but in sunnier lands it was lazy and fat.
Death's heads danced at the Mardi Gras,
their fatness eaten away.
Carni vale: goodbye to sins,
as well as to flesh.
In Rio, New Orleans,
Marseilles and Nice,
"parting is such sweet sorrow."

A little more sloth is the antidote
to all the destruction around us.
A sitting person seldom kills;
idle fingers pull few triggers;
sluggish minds invent no bomb.

Carnival may not cure
the miasma of Brazil,
but it does more good than bulldozers.

The managers call it sloth,
but I call it rest, an apercu,
opening up reality.
We're drugged on deadlines.
Sloth is a lifeline,
a field lying fallow,
nature in winter,
a snake on a rock in the sun,
a hound dog gnawing a bone,
a babe in the womb,
a child doodling dreams in the dust;
primal innocence,

playing at madness,
to forestall the ultimate
insanity of progress.

If I had the money I'd go to New Orleans,
but I don't, so I'll dream of Brazil,
where the weather is August,
and the bare bellied dancers
crowd closer.

The poor have a right to forget.

FREE ZONE

When school starts I'm glad.
It's the magic circle,
where I can rest,
where it's safe to say it;
the rules protect our enquiry.

We laugh together at the absurdity;
we know the circle is part illusion.
But we get inklings,
of reality and wonder.

Life is good and all is well,
this drowsy bumblebee afternoon.
The king will not be poisoned.

JAZZ US SOME LANGUAGE REVIVIFIED

Grammar is the death of language
not its living natured bones
grammar is the treatment
by centuries of quack doctors
on the body of the word
grammar is hypochondria
that picks away at style

Not Homer nor Hesiod nor Aeschylus
nor even subversive Socrates
were worried by grammar
but reveled in the fires of night
reflected in the eyes of their listeners
reveled in the hushed assembly
shaded by hill from afternoon sun
reveled in the give and take
of spontaneous argument

But Athens fell
and Sparta too
and death prevailed
and all of Plato s stratagems
could not save the body
political or literary
from the nit-picking scholars
he unwittingly invited

The mathematics of language
measures too many doses
too many remedies
too many bloody dissections

Jazz us away on winged words

from classics too closely remembered
to secret cauldrons and hidden waters
to uncharted winds
where inborn genius
is sparked to new life
by chance response
to improvised word
in celebration
large or small or intimate

Jazz us to the age-old rites
of Kelt and Bantu
and far Polynesian
of Slav and Hindi and Nipponese
of people gathered
in seemingly sterile
ethnic routine
of gatherings unsanctioned
by proper custom
of Voodoo mama and offbeat Odysseus
of wild Dionysus and Pilgrim maid
of potion salted by old Mother Earth
and stirred by the light of the moon

Of gatherings sanctioned
by ancient custom
where habitual language
turned new by the moment
is carelessly guided
by the ears of the elders
who sit on the sidelines
and delight in their dancing
and chanting young

Jazz us into the dazzling eye
of nature's whole
reality

COMFORT OF PUMPKINS

The roundness of pumpkins
brings promise of spring
their color will brighten the winter
I pick one carefully for its curves
and keep it under the TV
it softens the impact of news

pumpkins are as old as witches
as old as the moon
gifts of the goddess of plenty
we hollow her out
her fullness remains

tread lightly
tread lightly
the Mother is resting

A CITY BOY LOOKS AT NATURE

1.

We worry about the rats,
but take delight in the squirrels.

What schizophrenic God created them?
Or is the split in us?

2.
The hummingbird danced
a full three minutes
on the garden hose spray
in the sunlight.

3.
There may be no weeds in nature,
but it's hard to tend a garden,
when you're curious to see what blossoms
on every volunteer.

THIS URGE THIS ITCH

to be heard to be read admired applauded and publicized to have a book that leads to another another that leads to national acclaim to the canon of the authors to being a household name but one that's loved not mocked or despised this has to be some kind of sickness

that afflicts not just me but all kinds of others who flock to the readings to read and be heard I'll listen to you if you'll listen to me yours is not really all that interesting but I admire your guts and I don't want to hurt you especially I mean I don't want you to hurt me

he taught us Cicero's letters he rambled a lot but was interesting and one thing he said I've remembered that poetry is only written by people who're sick and it's mainly sick people read it

sometimes I think the writer's meetings I go to are kind of like therapy sessions we may not help one another get over our illness but we do help one another cope we work hard to keep up the illusion of something worthwhile being written and read

but you can say that for all conversation how much of it is really all that important maybe it can be an end in itself like ice cream or brandy it may not make us well but it sure makes us feel better so what's the harm if it helps us survive and occasionally thrive we'll have moments of wonder and glory we'll have memories to see us through

ON BEING UNPUBLISHED
AT FIFTY NINE

If I can't live forever
I want to be remembered
but grandchildren make their own
and their grandchildren?

what do I know of my great-grandparents?
a marble tombstone?
who will read it?
and if anyone does
will the name mean me?

these lines I am writing
I may never read them again myself
after a season or two

a public reading?
my wife may like them
a few friends
partisans
simpatico
may find some truth for the moment

T.S. Eliot
do you know you're still famous?
Robert Frost
did your demons die with you?
Emily Dickenson
do you hear the applause?

William Shakespeare
never heard of King Tut
did Tut enjoy his return to fame

after three thousand years
of anonymous safety?

master artists and rank apprentices
working promiscuously
left no names
on Chartres or Notre Dame
on Indian or African ceremonial
on creative winds
still blowing and stirring
boiling and brewing

that jazz that jive that gumbo
that electronic mumbo jumbo
that breathes nameless life
into our neatly labeled joints

changes changes e'endownst to same
what it is don't need no name

PLURIFORM WAYS
TO APPRECIATE POETRY

Some like it on the printed page
some like it better in bed
others prefer it performed on stage
still others will say instead

they get more excited
just to hear it recited
in rhythmic drone
of monotone
by a reader seemingly dead.

"A THING WORTH DOING IS WORTH DOING POORLY"

G.K.Chesterton

Most of us are mediocre most of the time; strive as we might we won't change it. Students can strain, and look better on paper; their scores will go up, but their knowledge will be superficial, a bother, a burden they will constantly need to escape.

School is supposed to mean leisure, a relaxed routine, but regular, steady. Accept it, it becomes a groove, and some of it gets interesting. We learn when we become curious; we gradually become adept, surprised by moments of

excellence,

> when the wind of the spirit
> turns work into play,
> the play becomes wisdom,
> and we're out of ourselves,
> and into the heart
> of the whole universal shebang.

A healthy acceptance of mediocrity, a measured joy in daily routine, might lead to a love of living, a kind of Franciscan spirit of poverty, a "give us this day" kind of sharing, a poetic relish of what's around us.

I'd like to market a new bumper sticker, one that reads something like this, "Happy parents of ordinary teenagers; their grades are low, but their spirits are high. They know that what counts cannot be counted."

THE TOOTH OF THE LION

Orchids will do
for special occasions
they're fine for the tropics
and people with hothouses

roses will always
set the standard
for gracious living
and careful gardening

there are hundreds of choices
at roadside nurseries

violets are available
but almost invisible

zinnias are what
we used to grow
hardy and cheap
for the 1930s

but nature's most extravagant gift
outrageously squandered
in sunlight and grass
is the dandelion

dent de lion
the tooth of the lion
millions on millions of miniature suns
glory spread golden and wide

the medieval French
those practical peasants

named the flower
for its edible leaf
jagged
like the tooth of the lion

but how did they know this?
did they know lions?
did they collect their teeth
and wear them like rabbits' feet?

maybe they learned from the Romans
from Christians whose friends
had been chewed by lions
were lions brought with the shows
to Marseilles and Nice and Arles
and the rest of Roman Provence?

the French made wine from the flower
and salad from the leaf

no field of California poppies
of Texas bluebonnets
or Indian paintbrushes
is more resplendent
than one spread golden
with dandelions

the glory is short
in a week they have faded
to wisps of silvery gray
not so attractive

but this is the time
to treat small children
to a parachute festival
pluck the wisps
throw them
watch them sail on the wind

an ephemeral flotilla
ready to land
and wait next year's resurrection

sometimes I wish
I were not schizophrenic
I wish I still felt as a child
more consistently

delight though I do
in dandelions
I can't stand them in my front yard
they disturb the Puritan esthetic
I pull them quickly before they can bloom
to spread their unorthodox glory

the adult tyrannizes the child
the lion the leaf and custom
have teeth

BY ANY OTHER NAME

"Would you pass the red jelly?"
my hostess asked
but I only saw green orange and purple

I passed her some purple
she said "No not the purple the red"
so I passed her the orange

she said "Thank you that's it"

a few minutes later
her husband asked me
to pass the red jelly

I passed him the orange
he said "No not the orange the red"
so I passed him the purple

he said "That's right thanks"

GIVE US THIS DAY

If I have a loaf of bread
and my brother my sister have none
then I owe them half
even if they do have a gun

I just might not realize
how much guns had to do
with my having the bread
in the first place

JESUS AIN'T NO

"Jesus" ain't no holy card name.
"Jesus" ain't no holy water name.
"Jesus" ain't no stained glass window name.

"Jesus" is Yasha, Yeshu,
Joshua, Jesse, Hesús,
an ordinary street name.

But would you want a dirty little kid like that
moving next door to you?
Would you want that wandering Jewish carpenter family
moving next door to you?

Well, maybe just one family, O.K.,
but then the whole tribe might try to follow,
and first thing you know,
the Jews would be taking over.
Samaritans too; they're worse you know.

And those strange foreign egghead magi,
and dumb shepherd types.

Then before long
the bog-trotting Irish,
with their pigs in the parlor,
would push in,

and what would happen
to our Klean Khristian Kommunity?

Yeshu, Baby,
crying in the straw,
be a stumbling block
a scandal,
that bumps us into reality.

THE OLD LADY'S HOUSE

The old lady's house seems empty
I see no lights
maybe a dim one halfway back
but I can't be sure

the geraniums in the window
are not as red and full as they used to be
and the ivy grown yard is a little more unkempt
than usual

I used to see her walking the cat
moving slowly with a cane
sitting on the front porch reading

sometimes I saw an old man there
and another old lady

last year there were younger visitors
someone must have been ill

crocuses and tiny stars
peep up every spring in her yard
the earliest of any I see
the woodsy green
the hospitable porch
the reading lamp by the window

I've walked by there almost every week
for several years now
every time I go to the bookstores nearby

old lady whoever whatever wherever
you are or have been or will be
oh may it be good and good and good

may your spirit live on forever
in crocuses and springtime
in warm light for reading
on winter nights

AT THE SEASIDE WITH MONET

Art Institute, 8-8-87

Suleyman the Magnificent
1520-1566
intricate flowery designs

Picasso's sketch books
he plays a lot
he loves life
it's contagious

but I still like the impressionists best
especially Monet's bluffs
looking out to the sea
on a sunny summer day

there's a breeze
sailboats
whitecaps
flowers in tall grass
two ladies
one with a parasol

it reminds me of the bluff
on Strawberry Island
the seminary retreat

but there were no ladies with parasols there

I'd like to live in this picture forever
but Monet is gone
the ladies are gone
the bluff has likely eroded

I'll soon be gone
but I d like to live forever

GOOD FRIDAY

April 1, 1988

A fool, for Christ s sake, the folly of my anger,
dragging the reluctant pup out the car door so impatiently that
his leg gets sprained and I make myself late to Chicago, having
to wait at the vet's an hour just to have him say the dog needs
no treatment but rest, and I have to shell out ten dollars anyway,
and by the time I'm looking for my regular place to park all the
spaces are taken, and when I check the parking lots they're all at
least five dollars, so I decide to look for a meter on the near
North, but the available ones are all for two hours limit, so I
look farther west and north and finally park free in a rundown
area under the el, where I surreptitiously take a pee, cautiously
recheck the car doors, and hurry on foot towards North
Michigan, where the Stations of the Cross have already started.

It's cold, but not painfully. I try to compose my
thoughts, remembering so many Good Fridays, and what I
learned and used to believe about the death of Jesus, and
wondering how much I still believe, but knowing the deepest of
anything I've ever known (believed?) that the life and death of
each individual person in Nicaragua Salvador Vietnam Ireland
Libya Lebanon Houston Chicago South Africa anywhere
anytime any way any reason or lack of reason is supremely
important, and the Buddhist Hindu Muslim Jewish Pagan
Agnostic Christian even Atheistic people who learn to respect
and try to help other people even the ones who are different
even the ones labeled enemy are the people who show the
hidden God to the world to me to you to them to our children,
and all these foolish believers on this walk the middle class ones
from the suburbs the middle class ones from the city the middle
class Blacks and Orientals, the middle class refugees from
Central America (everybody on the walk looked middle class),
all these insignificant few at least give symbolic recognition to
the suffering of so many and the heroism of some and the

mystery of the hope of prisoners and widows and orphans and veterans and sick and hungry and wounded, the hope and joy and humor and stubborn every day keeping on of people in barrios and ghettoes, in schools and streets and offices, in neighborhoods and non-neighborhoods of every class and description.

Between wisdom and folly ain't that much difference, and when we are not afraid to be fools could be when we're wise.

And daffodils say there just might be some kind of Hallelujah that really gives meaning to all this foolishness.